About That

Written by Audacious Don

Table of Content:

* Favorites

* Favorites

Introduction

Fear is a MOTHERFUCKA

It will keep you in your house, stuck in your room and scare you out of doing what you know you need to do. But once you accomplish a little a at time, the after feeling is like breathing out a burden. During this moment, your stomach aches, you get anxiety, start over thinking, but once you're done, you're all like "that's it?" And laugh at yourself. Laugh at the crazy, unrealistic imagination you had beforehand. Applaud your baby steps and big girl/big boy steps. This is a part of growing up. This is Life. It's unexpected, spontaneous, and you can only control so much of it, but that's okay. It is what it is. And it's all about the rest of the day what you do with it. Knock out the hard stuff, then treat yourself to something free or something worthwhile. Take a mental note because you may come back to this uncomfortable gut feeling again. But remember... You have before. You made it before. You're a BEAST!

Hands-Free

I need my fix.
Can't live without it.
Can't go "Live" without it,
"Tony! Toni! Toné!" is my ringtone,
    phone lays on my pillow,
        I'm more available to this device that the people saved in it,
            but.....who's really safe in it?

Face gorilla glued to its hypnotizing, enticing flash lights, icons and apps,
I've adapted to hearing notifications,
I'm a trained slave running fast to it,
Sitting in AA, Apps Anonymous because it's a must I quit this electronic habit,

How can this phone create more connection yet everyone's distance?
For instance, I've considered a family plan but Alcatel, I mean, I can tell,
    it'll still be silence, hearing Cricket,

This addiction is risky,
Motorola while my motors running,
Can't help but text and drive,

I didn't know I had a problem,
Wish someone could've pulled me to the side,
But no one will because this drug has kept everyone high, nationwide,
    unaware of Proposition 65,

And yet I keep roaming towards my 5G pusher,
Steady abusing my data usage,
WIFI, I mean, why fight it?
Because we all do it,

The emergency emerged in me when this simple rectangle strangled my common sense,
  Losing grip of consequence,
    Since the moment my wrist flinched,
      Phone dived off my hand like swimming Olympics,
I'm reaching out to save my saved apps, bank account, contacts,
  MY WHOLE LIFE IS IN IT,
    So attached I lost track of the tracks, I'm a magnet to my phone,
    forgetting the train's horn blowing in the back,
Smash, Crash, CRACKED like a phone screen, I SCREAM.....
    Swiped left by a bigger machine because of this hand-held thing,
      Just another victim
        who let their carrier
          bury her.

Admitting Is The First Step

She just... Keeps creating distractions,
Not use to unloading emotional baggage,
Not the Badu song type because she isn't carrying it at all,
  Like she flys hands-free yet too scared to fall,
    Not in love but fall on her face,
      Or her face wet from crying on a man,
And he's just trying to understand why she's not open,
But she demands and acts out in anger when indeed she's sad,
Hurts more because he's by far the best man she's ever had,
But he won't hear those words cuz she keeps her heart guarded,
Starving her black roses in a waterless garden,
Drought in her harvest from constantly being heartless,
Scared to show her true face behind that smiling mask when in reality she's crying,
    But when her heart starts up again like a cold machine.....
      Her brain says "Hey, look over here instead",
Exchanged feelings for numbness to avoid another heart break again,
Fear of the unknown,
  Scared of not knowing what may happen,
    So she avoids getting captured,
      By his watery eyes that submit,
By his meaningful "I love you's" that don't quit,
And she cringes and questions his love everytime he says "You're so perfect",
She just scratches her head, face twisted,
  Stubborn to admit that,
    She, too, wants to openly love him as much as he deserves it,
But since she can't see where this love could be going..... She just sits.........
  Like an awaiting passenger on a bus stop bench,
But keeps letting transportation pass by, cuz getting too emotional is a trip,
  And she sees weakness in crying,
    Yet He needs to know this,
      She needs to show this,
        To cry into each other arms vulnerably explosive,
"Please convince me pain's actually over and it's okay to be held,
Help soften a harden heart that I never used well".

After These Messages

Once upon a time,
And then happily ever after,
Scenes of slow motion running,
Noses touch then lips,
Soft kiss and love at first sights,

Main character face challenges then overcome,
Person starts poor then suddenly rich,
End of each movie ending with hope, because that's what Hollywood pitches,
...... And I used to be into it.....
Believing in second, third, fourth chances,
Quick, uncomplicated romances,
Sad moments with good sweet endings,
Just all the pretending,
Until I grew up,
Got older,
And reality started unpeeling,
So after all of the real heartbreaks from relationships, family losses, and debt,
Life became very unappealing,
Started fishing for answers but wasn't much I could reel in,
And people suggest "well, this is just life, really",
But as the floor rose higher and ceiling came closer,
It was like I wasn't given the chance to heal, get comfort and find closure,
Like a baby out of the womb, I'm in a room called Life with too much exposure,
Then I learned to fall in love with movies again

Seeing a new meaning to films that use to seem corny but they were temporary fixes,
Because life's not a TV where if you don't like what it is, like a channel, just try to switch it,
So I travel through movies where the boy gets it all in the end or the lovers divided find another again,
Seeing the lonely girl with no family finding true family through close friends,
Just gripping the remote cuz at least I can control this...... Even when my life goes out of whack,
Watching shows I use to as kid so much, like I'm desperate to get my childhood back.

Better Now Than Never

We make too many deadlines as we grow older.
Assuming that my time to shine would've been an explosion if I started this
  dream younger,
But my timeline doesn't define how soon I should start because I had growth
  to sort through.
So although I may make it after hitting past my thirties, I flirt more with the
  idea of exploring how the teenage Me was col'...... But now I'm older, crisp
  and colder.
Playing with open mics and entertaining family and friends,
Now I'm networking because I measured my worth and,
I see I could be the new buzz nowadays,
Sober the buzzed with wordplay,
Turn my work into pay,
Retail's a dead end but my life begins when I say,
So,
Watch me bloom and don't assume I'm late, based off my age, that's insane.
Compare me to the greats, who accomplished previous things before life
  Granted opportunity,
Starting today I'm changing my perspective,
Like if my life was an old resume, I updated my objective,
Bounce back well when rejected, but treat it like a job and punch in daily,
Sometimes miss my lunch break for the dream I'm chasing,
Putting in overtime! Never go slow!
Unless I finally make it to where I want to be then I'll use my PTO,
Big dreaming like my goals on swole like the hulk carrying a bulk of
  success,
And even by then.......I ain't done yet,
Like my soul never heard the word "No",
  so I keep putting in work till I get a "Yes",

Treat the life like Checkers,
No, Chess,
Or invest until I own property, money stack high and sloppy, catch me
wearing a top hat
  Like dude from Monopoly,
Live like there's no limit to my greatness so I explore SUCH ,
Ignore negativity, and give no........apologies.

Cheers To You

This isn't like me,
This isn't familiar.
Battling a dog with bark and no bite
  But now suddenly wanna fight, to play "father-figure",
Well that's a bitch move and No, I don't feel ya,
Involving the law with a tucked tail,
  Like a tattle-tale treating your honor like he's your father,
Crying "She won't let me see my son" when you know damn well that ain't
  the problem,
Tell them the truth like how you denied him being yours and there was no
  where to find you,
How you hide from responsibilities forcing me to be super mama.
Ditched a huge hospital bill on me but you promised you got him,
Our son almost went without a crib, you said my current boyfriend could've
  solved it,
Like you wake up revengeful instead of focusing on your seed,
You mad you became the parent you despised, neglectful as she,
So now you're left to hate all women, even if your son's mother is me,

Now I'm stuck with a immature imbecile with unresolved child issues,
So unhappy with your life, you pull everyone into it,
Got me thinking as cold hearted as you but, this isn't like me.
This isn't familiar.
I was never a petty person picking at weaknesses like a starving vulture,
Tugging at the unsuspecting prey's flesh like emotionally abusing others,
  Satisfies your hunger,
But with one eye open,
As I may sit in my own blood, just know that......I ain't dead..... And what
  doesn't kill me...... Only makes me stronger.

False Believes

Believe me,
You are not needed,
Necessary,
A necessity,
Even though you seem as sweet,
as Nestle,
But heart is darker than the skin on Westley,
Sniping at your girl's mental,
Like I'm suppose to believe that what we have is natural,
But,
Believe me,
I got this thing here,
Stay out my bubble, boy,
Messing with these dudes ain't nothing but trouble, boy,
Trying to take this lady,
And rough her up with a muzzle, boy,
To toys, you can, but me, don't play,
Because I'll discombobulate you like a puzzle, DOH!!!

I need to be loyal to me first and foremost,
Who are you to enjoy my presence, and essence,
I'm no goddess,
Though my existence is a blessing,
Being a people-pleaser will piss me off and only leave me restless,
And breathless,
And careless,
Incautious enough to take danger and face it,
Thirsty and anxious,
Anxious or thirsty,
Quench my thirst of being let down
with three glasses of "I'm sorry",
Spiked with shots of "not calling",
Which overflows to the wrong thing,
Misleading me to believe you,
But why, shoot!

Believe me,
The theory of you being of importance,
  Is a hypothesis dissected into sections of wasted apologies,
You in my Biology is Prehistoric Science,
Believing in you was like dealing with a dude who won't DO, cuz he stuck in
  TRYING,
Pausing my life for a lost cause who,
Crawls across my drawn lines,
Cute face and characteristics,
Aren't enough to hold my attention,

I mastered surpassing diseasters,
So I pass you in silence.

For Momma

If music represents the heart,
Then you're a record player broken,
Fixable but unfortunate to repeat the same song, on repeat, repeat,
Never fully playing out til it gets to the best part,
Same beat, and a reckless rhythm of confusion,
Dillusional enough to believe it's always someone else's hip that hit your
record player,
Someone's hit emotionally and spiritually is to blame so for the insane,
   That claims everyone who has done their natural part are to blame,
Yeah that's an answer you've grown secure in,
Enduring a snake being a snake because you've mistaken,
    Mistake it as rope hanging there,
      Dangling to pull you from disdain you bare,
        But it pains you there,
          Here, in your broken heart-like record,
            To grow sight of what was always a sly snake swaying from the sky,
             Disguised for yet another quench fulfilling bite,
Same as those who repeatedly lie to you,
Can't even distinguish between them and those who sincerely love you,
And then sometimes there are times you hurt so much that I am only able to
   look at you,
Hoping to symbolically see through,
See your music Maker and grab the needle that constantly scratches,
But my hand, you always smack then return to back to your bad habit,
By replacing the needle back, then
Replacing yourself back in,
Situations that leave you gasping,
Questioning what happen,
The " How did I get here?",
Because you always wait to feel hurt only after you've snapped then,
Then left hoarse, hardly heard, and unhappy,
Almost too independent with your sadness even when a helping hand is
asking,

You've had enough distraction,

Action is now axing at your door for you to dig deep and correct the caused scars that never healed,

Take the wheel of your life,

Take a knife and cut ties with bless-blocking situations and leech-like people,

Go from "settling" to "saving" yourself while you have enough left of you, and your mind...... And especially your spirit.

Guess Who's Coming To Dinner

I am the worst company to keep,
I over stay my welcome,
I drain your energy, leave you empty,
You're welcome,
Seldom do I sleep,
I sneak in when you're lonely,
Celebrating isolation,

I'm so good at my job,
You'll beg for medication,
You'll beg to be sedated after I make your mind hate you,
I feed off negativity and your depression is very tasteful,
I'm a mystery,
You can feel me but can't see me,
You can't tell friends or family,
Because I'll make you sound crazy when you're explaining,
Seducing you with illusion of lies,
I'm stitched in between each and every thought,
I clock in, rarely punch out, I prefer overtime,
Now others think they've seen me,
Like when they get fired or someone dies,
Maybe thought I was that sad feeling when a marriage feels deprived,
But oh no, I attack and attach at all times, on an all time high, disgustingly
disguised, Jump out SURPRISE when you're feeling your finest,

When you're holding your baby,
I numb that.
When you're invited out,
I numb that.
Your favorite movies are a dull black and white static because guess what?
I've already attacked it,

And I last for years,
A sweet chemical brain imbalance,
I challenge the optimistic,
I laugh at your attempts,
If emptiness is a winning prize,
Here's a chest pain trophy plus nice slit wrist,
See I disturb those who don't get me,
But to the depressed, they get my messy message,
I'm the worst company to keep.....
And the wrong mental illness to mess with.

Holiday

Holding another obituary........
Scary how rarely life's taken for granted, family and friends taken from rapidly, I panic,
And here creates our "Family Reunion"....
Only to see faces who reside close by or further but only if we lose....
Another.
And it's sickening.
The psychology of like-minds mourning separately,
Feeling like our tears are a burden,
Like we're under a curse but unknowingly choose to lose cuz we're creating our own antidotes..... Selfishly.
And the potion concocted won't work because YOU got an ingredient I need,
But since we not talking, our antidotes are worthless,
So hurt, we're blind,
So devastated, time passes,
So oblivious to the living walking right pass us,
Forwarding their calls,
Ignoring family cuz we harvest guilt, confusion, and blame,
Unaware that with each passing death we do the same thing, just wave at each other
   Saying, "I see you next funeral" like we birthed a cursed holiday.....
In only making time when time's up,......
The clock's big and small hand applauding our insanity to repeat the same things and expecting different outcome,
HOW COME you can't come out and hold me now?
Rather wait to hover over my shell, in a permanent bed amongst others mourning?
This is a challenge of weathering a storm, man,
Instead of keeping your weeping stored in, not letting it free but letting more in,
Keeping score of the worst days, "How many days since last incident?", like it's our job
   Or only focus,

I wanna laugh, vent, bond, but everybody's not MAKING it important,
Prioritizing family more often,
And this is what I'm taking from this....

Are there not enough good memories to overshadow the bad?
Is Death THAT much stronger than Life that we choose to mourn more than
make new memories?
Is it just me who feel these thoughts,
Taught to sweep feelings under the rug, shoulder shrug, appear numb when
    really a loud cry of hopelessness hums a demonic tune in my soul,
Begging me to give up and give in.....
But you know what?.....
That ain't the way our cloth is cut!
So just a little at a time with no excuses, I'll come see how you doing,
Kick it, play cards, crack jokes how I'm losing,
Make a dish or bring the drinks, whatever or just show up,
Laugh so hard I cry, stomach tight cuz you funny as ever,
Dance or sing together a song that takes us back,
Proactive with interaction instead of acting like we're too busy,
And yeah my persuasive game is strong yet I make excuses sometimes too,
Hopefully whoever I reach can make the first step as I made the first words,
Being with family CAN give you a form of healing,
You just gotta do the work.

It Was All Worth It

The multiple nurses fade, pain becomes a haze,
Overbearing sweat lightens after sight of you....
And this time, like the first and last time,...
It was all worth it

A common quote numerous mothers spill while tears block sight but
spirituality I'm
  Holding you,
A bond long overdue, waited for what seemed like a forever,
Up to 9 months from shock I'll be having you, to denial if I'm ready, if I'm
  the right mom Because it's my first time,
No one REALLY knows how to master the power of Parenting,
    And yet behold me,
I hold a curious little version of me who makes me feel like I'll be the best
  damn mom Unconditionally loved,
    probably even love me more than I love myself,
Some mothers see babies as a wrench in their lifestyle but you're my
  upgrade,
    my blessing, my new beginning, my second chance, my motivation when
      no one can reach me and all you do is smile, coo and cry,
Nights of no sleep, me learning to walk, heal from stitches which is a pain so
ridiculous,
  Signing multiple hospital documents while under pain meds and I.V. , learn
everything here before being released to go home trust me I'm trying,
And when people hear my war story of Hick-like Braxtons, multiple
  contractions,
    Excruciating pain attacking my lower back and seeing the blood, the
      baby, wondering what's my reaction and it's always the same tear-filled
        joyful answer......
It was all worth it,
And you're my second child,
My princess in addition to your older royal brother,
Still I would have it no other way and would do it again.

Knock On Wood

Pinocchio,.....Naw,
Pino-negro.
Played like a puppet in America,
Stringing us along to believe we're truly free but I recognize lies, believe me, because
Their nose always grows,...
And below me is a stage where I perform daily like slavery, no pay, so they're just playing me, and
No matter how great my performance they throw bullets like tomatoes,
Never good enough,
Ever since I was created, they hover over me a cross that's contagious in spreading fear through spiritual lies like low key Bible bangers,
Obliviously waiting on blue eyed Jesus to save us,
And don't tell them they came from us cuz they'll deny the true creator,
We are mahogany colored trees but these new sheets don't get us,
My brown skin threatens these sheets so they simply want to rid us,
In denial, call us primal, but the truth is in us .... In DNA..... In true human
  evolution, NOT MONKEY BUSINESS,
But I am just Pino-negro.... Walking these paths, screaming to the mass
  "I'm a REAL Boy" with hands up DON'T SHOOT,
Almost begging to be treated equally,
Almost crying to be seen as human,
But inevitably, always dying like a dog,

Though my Gipetto keeps me strong helping me cope with modern society and their cave man ways,
Can't even joke about death, so I branch towards knocking on wood often to soften the blow that could happen,
I'm simply a carved boy puppet trying to be conscious, and some black ladies are misguided too to be honest,
Like my friend Sleepy Beauty awaiting a kiss from a Woke Black Prince,
But some are content,
Don't want to be pinched to wake up to reality,
But no, not me,......I see reasons to be mentally free, learned beyond
    stereotypes and choose to be unique rather than in sync with society,
        almost mystique,

Tired of singing Let Freedom Ring,
Now my new song is I've Got No Strings.

Semi-colon

I gotta get this tattoo.... Semicolon,
Something to hold on to,
Semicolon to keep me going,
I'm just strolling through social media,
Crying behind a face, man,
Hiding behind filters,
Brain is just programed to feel guilty,
Wishy washy with my ambition, I just wish I knew what I wanted,
This endless emptiness taunts me,
24/7 numbness,
Haunted through daylight, can't catch a break when I snooze,
Since I lose in my dreams or have insomnia,
So really let me ask you something?
Last time I checked,
My life hadn't had childhood trauma,
Or did I black out something horrible,
Question is "How can the ones I know suffering similarly to me had multiple
Hells on earth happen but I can't grasp a past to unravel why I'm messed up
in the brain aisle?"
Too many *Hows* and *Why Me*,
    I can't seem to connect why I'm hurting worse than the next,
Putting effort in pills, therapy and books trying to study my madness,
Having to dissect why I despise rejection and never can complete a task,
How is it that even at a workplace I still have panic attacks,
There's a war brewing between my spirit and mind,
So remind me what it's like to win,
And with all this people respond with "Well just think positive!"
    Now why didn't I think of this,
These are the comments that put my mind in coma-mode, locked down like a
    prison,
My last bit of hope lines on a period above a comma,
Because everything else that once was real to me, has lost meaning to be
    honest.

Speak Slow

This is not all that you are.
You were born for better, and
Even though lately you haven't felt your best, you are meant for greatness....
    And nothing less.

You are that shyness of a twinkle that blends into the dark night's sky,
With the potential to burn eyes if you blare more often, just shine loudly,
blind eyes and make those who speak of you as a star recognize you're truly a
Sun.
But to be a Sun..... to even... be one, you have to breathe......,
Oxygen is just one of the ingredients.
Take a deep breath and exhale greatness like rays and hope it scorches the
envious nay-sayers.

Don't wait for a hero,
Don't sit until a blessing approaches,
Live limitless like life's a game without planning to lose.
Choose you living amongst the dream you dreamt you deserve and smile
through it naturally.
Tell yourself "Happiness is meant for me".

Find silver linings through sad times, shout your blessings outloud,
Stack enough *hope* to cash in to receive blessings, bit by bit, or by abundance
so overwhelming because no battle like this is fit for small soldiers,
It's a tall order but you got the ingredients,
God won't ever put weight you can't bare on your shoulders,
He sees what you don't.
He sees your strength.

Terrible Twos

I'm trying.
Better yet I'm down,
Down on one knee,
Gripping my lace,
Heart at a fast pace,
Prepping to race,
At the starting line,
Despise my circumstances standing in front of me,
I've summoned a stronger *me* like those imaginative card games,
Claim the trophy before lifting a finger,
Lifting my own chin up,
Lifting my spirit,
Choosing to save myself.
Choosing to take baby steps till I'm a top notch toddler because I'm prepared for the terrible twos: Anxiety and Depression.
Learning daily to end my obsession with aggressively blaming myself for not healing overnight because....that's not right.
Learning to give myself credit when it's due.. even if I'm emotionally in debt,
I crept out of this hole of pity and hopelessness and I just hope this is my last sad poem, because my family and friends I owe them.....
Owe them a chance to understand me on this earth rather than confused if I dropped dead,
But honestly.... That's not where my heart is.
I wanna be here!
I wanna live life like crazy, it's just that for the time being I'm fighting my mind and she's mean,
She's been harsh and relentless so I have unfinished business I'm attending to end this!
No...... Not my life..... End this madness.
Cuz there is a cure,
I'm having hope,
I must trust my dopeness.

Up For It

Here we are back again,
Convincing me to draw back into a comfortable spot of idleness,
Avoiding the tongue biting because the next harsh words I spit could cut
deeper than a
   Knife, it's sick,
Dealing with an ill minded man who contradicts,
Starting to see the real ill in you that really made your past lovers quit,
Déjà vu for you but I'm just a new character,
Who barely holds substance, while you're boisterous under substance,
Or intoxicated, so I'm just some blurr to you, who can't get through to you,
Like I'm shoving through a crowd of strangers,
   That's how much I don't notice you,
Can't recognize the man I thought I loved,
What has come over you?
I told myself I wouldn't waste my time getting into love if from my man,
   It's been past due,
So I ask you,
Is this the game of who hurts worst because I could pass you,
I'm someone on your egg shells cuz settling defines you,
Done with metaphorical jail cells, being confide to tell you everything on my
   mind in every argument excelled, since it'll only raise hell in this kitchen,
     and you ain't ready for that dish,
My plate is overwhelmed, and you add bits of tasteless things on it,
The ship sailed for second chances, because there's a "We" in "wedding" but
neither "I"
   Or "you" in forever,
This reflection shows unnecessary recklessness,
Trust gets thinner every time I check my check list,
I've dealt with garbage before but can't afford anymore messes,
I'm doing for you what's new for me, I use to be horrible, just ask my exes,
You've been closed off, there's no key I have that can fix this,
I've been pulling my end, where's your end of this bargain,
Me asking you to open up shouldn't be a bother, when you're the one who
   wanted a marriage,

Well keep up the good work,
I rather keep learning early for what I'm signing up for,
Long term's looking like a dead end,
What are you in this for?

Family Tribute

I'm hurt that you're gone,
Left too soon without goodbyes,
Too soon to say sorry for not enough time spent with you,
To embrace your spirit, smile, and laughter,
God, just to catch one last glimpse of you,
To have cheers, just one last sip with you,
And for the younger one....... to see you bloom into an astounding woman, to have the chance to say " Proud of you",
Now the clouds gloom to the lack of all of you,
Anger urges my soul to avenge you,
But in knowing how sweet you were you would tell me to be stronger and I know better, then lift me up with a joke or two,
God there's no length of both arms stretched out to explain how wide my love is for you,
Not a blueprint of a skyscraper or pyramid to mimic how high my love is for you,
Love so overwhelming even these words from my quivering weak jaw, lump in my throat can barely dive off my lips into this page to save this family I hope there's enough beauty to describe of you,
Illustrating your life and impact on me and them and those admiring our family,
They wonder how are we so multitalented, humble and high spirited but it flows through our veins naturally,
But trying to deal with what is happening,
How you all were selfishly snatched from us rapidly,

I know I have to stop and remember that....... this is God working on us so be silent and listen.

Listen how hard He roars in our ears to gather more often for happier occasion,
Yeah it hurts deep but God is DEEP too...look at *His* persuasion,
Telling us to enjoy the company of those who've been here and continue or pass down family tradition,

Celebrate more often and make time to see each other like you know it could be the last day rather than wait until their last days,
Release grudges and just hug me, Please!! because life's not promised,
Don't just tag me, dial me, hear my voice on the other end, check on me once in while,
Our family is too beautiful to feel alone individually or left out,
Be considerate and reach out to the extended, because the ones we keep losing would want that even if it wasn't verbally admitted.......
Let's just love for a minute, please....
And unfortunately the love we can no longer give to the deceased, let's overwhelm that same love and energy, to those who still walk amongst us now, you see,
We need to exchange the guilt, hurt, the "I should've been theres" to being there now for each other,
It's hard, but God heals,
Take each day at a time,
I know that terrifying feeling,
I can testify,
It's that.....
Pulsating energy behind my sternum,
Stun in the rib cage,
Constant pain takes over leaving less breaths to take,
Can't even fake a smile, these paths become ongoing miles,

Cracked grounds like weak backs calasping beneathe so see how I can't stand,
Like I'm in Hell's circus tight-roping with the last hope in the hospital,

I told her I wanna hold her,
Awaiting her return if she's strong enough to pull through,
Understanding this is her battle between her and God,
So she also needs hope from you,
Let's reach out and not fight this sadness alone,
And constantly hold memories dear,
We'll miss you all my loves,
But your spirit is still here.

Lady Luck

I get overlooked,
Misunderstood,
Looking for Lady Luck because I'm lacking,
Need to be pushed off a cliff into millions of four-leaf clovers,
Because I've been conned by the leprechaun ten times over,
What's being sober, when drunk thoughts leave you more open,
Left with a dry smile on an island surrounded by a hopeful ocean,
But in order to swim, I got to take a leap,
Courage don't come cheap, pockets on empty,
Turn them inside-out, you're on the outside looking in,
I'm like a building burning down, you're like "It's not that bad",
As if this is a bed I made to lie in,
This is a heartbreak hotel, I ain't never check in,
I'm the student in the back of the class with my left hand holding my right
  arm, right hand up for affection, not attention,

A white flag in a war on myself but everyone's battling their own messes,
Like a key to a socket in the wall, that's how much I fit in,
God's my only crutch when life's to much to mess with,
He said there's a message and a method to this madness,
So since I'm insane in the membrane,
  Nut case,
    Empty headspace,
      Head case,
        Screw loose,
          Then I should have a clue to what's next then,
That in the end I'll win...if the pressure doesn't break me first,
If the depression doesn't get worse,
This challenging road is unpredictable,
  Never got the chance to rehearse,
    Live life to the fullest or leave in a hearse,

Despite those who disqualify my hurt and say "It could be worse",
Shit on my pity with sarcastic bits with wit then split on me when I'm too
   much,
The world couldn't stomach me either so mother nature spit me up,
But instead of letting this pain stay intrusive,
I will face my fears in hopes to find the truth in,
   the damage that can be rebuilt, God is my toolkit,
Knocking a few letters from the words "Don't Quit",
And summoning something strong in me that whispers "Do It",
The devil playing the flute and I got to face the music,
He knocking me further down while I'm at my lowest,
I need silence and peace away from his noises,
I gotta fight this over and over and OVER again because I'm left with less
   choices,
I was too in tune to his gloom,
But now I'm hearing my own voice,
Its saying " A battle this huge fits me because I've been chosen",
Master my mistakes then move on,
Tell the pain to be gone,
To win this time and to be strong the next time the storm hits,
To push passed your limits, you never knew you had,
To let go, to let God,
Enjoy peace because this fight never ends.

Loving a Stranger

What defines a man?
Is it a woman's house with a stained tiolet unflushed because the extra step's
too much,
Is it the beer cans, old food stuck on plates next to the trash bin but not in,
The struggle of his days end in nights of isolation clinging to his game
controller when his woman has a policy of open doors,
Simply an ear to spare for a man's shut mouth and closed mind,
In due time, the end closes in and only then he'll see bags packed and empty
    closets,
From half a relationship that relied on two participating,
But his own needs blinded him and robbed her patience,
Her stomach ached from swallowing repeated promises of "I would never"
    And " I'm trying",
It always end with someone exploding with anger and someone else crying,
Complacency at its best verses compromising,
Like playing a game you'll never win and expecting prizes,

She sees the smoke as warnings but he's not woke until he's stuck in fire,
She tries fixing problems based of reoccuring predictions,
    But to him she's nagging and crying,
She's holding on to who he use to,
    Needs to be,
      Promises to be,
        But they'll never be,
Because one person pushes purpose and growth,
    While the other is just planted,
      Sort of like a couch potatoe,
        Like the joke of having too many eyes but can't see,
          Unaware of what surrounds him,
            Unalert the house is emptying,
              Confusing love with comfort,....
                Confuse confrontation from her as anger,
                  Overlooking that she's fighting and who's slowly becomes a
                    Stranger.

Her Forced Story

You can't force a new beginning,
It's just not ready for you,
More like not trying to make the 1 you into 2,
And you're not the only one going through,
  The breakup B.S.,
You're sitting on the side,
  Being his side to feel big,
    But it's nothing but your ego,
      Trying to feed its appetite,
As much as you want to let go,
  The strength of your conscience isn't right,
    So at night you cool your temper, your bitterness, your empty feeling,
      To get a moment, because you're lonely,
        from a guy who just wants to get it,
You may seem cool with that,
  But you're hurting, your face shows it,
    This stranger isn't a back patter,
      Or says "You're beautiful" when you're glowing,
      He won't help you advance from your past,
Honestly, to you, he's straight boring,
  But you'll keep him overnight,
    And imagine he's your boyfriend in the morning,

It's really that simple,
Despite his smile, funny jokes and cute dimples,
You'll settle for anything to fill that hole that's in the middle,
The one that's in your heart,
  And best believe below too,
When guys spot your head is hung low,
They're definitely gonna play you,
And those that aren't dogs are going to say,
  "Wonder what she'd been through?"
Don't wonder what I've seen, did, or do,
I'm trying to run from my shadow,
Seems crazy but you'd do the same when you try to leave your problems,
My heart's that broken bottle you witnessed,
It was tossed in the air for laughter,
Then fell fast, fell in love, fell heart-first then shattered,
Now everytime I hear his name, it hits me in the blatter,
Now I carry a long face, can't explain what's the matter,
I risk it all and everything for an hour in which a dude showers,
  admiration in my ear, as he's on top of me,
Nights that could've resulted in disease or pregnancy,
  Just for a misled lady who yearns ecstacy,
    Even if two X's replaces her eyes,
      And a coffin is her bed,
        All is left of her is a sad story,

Story of ignorance, story of lust,
Story of where was her father,
Chapter 1 called "The Girl Who Loved Love",
First paragraph of who she blames,
First sentence of childhood lane,
Back of the book reflects her indifferent face,
Published in her older days,
Watch her fade,
Notice her image become thin,
Grey-haired elder woman,
Telling teens her story again,
And again,
   Again,
    Again,
     Again until,
Thee End.

But Wait

Kiss me.
But kiss me, here, on the forehead,
Hold my hand, say you miss me,
Do what he did but better until I'm convinced,
  That I'm over him,
And when under you, I'll dare to catch your eyes,
Even if you don't bother to see mine,
When I whine, tell me it's okay, fine and dandy,
Tell me "If I were your man..." things,
Don't make me feel,
Just make me,
Don't place your index under my chin, lift it up, close your eyes, come close,
  Then let me fall,
Present your heart to me or nothing at all,
Bitterness leaves me picky,
   Want someone to do something like pick me in a crowd of cactus,
    So I'd feel like a "bad bitch",
Then rotate the sand into a place of pleasure, paradise, and hold me for about
mmm...
   Forever,
Fill my needs as quickly as I fill my wine glass,
  And don't ask questions but be my answer,
Say it's okay to move fast even though us joining will be a disaster,
Give me a reason to be glad I have you,
Finally when it's over,
I'd know then I'd be sober,
Mind dizzy from many thoughts,....or.....at least I think,
Hurry before our end is near,
Don't wait until the eye blinks,
Take me back to where we began,
  Or simply take me, before you don't exist,

Remind me of the feel of your lips,
  And right where we stand, I want you to kiss me,
    Just once again on my forehead,
      Just like how he once did,
But wait.....you're not him.

It Gets Better

It gets better,
Pain becomes less than,
  Before,
Like the actual energy of pain gets weak.
With all things in life,
Not everything last so it ceases,
Giving you again breaths to breathe,
  Happiness to reach,
    Learn these patterns by
     Taking notes and taking heed,
       Taking my example I endure and see,
Please just see how......it gets better,

Aw yeah, it's coming to me now,
How repetitious life can be,
Sometimes it's vicious but puts us back here again,
"I'm back here AGAIN!? Damn",
Back to needing a friend,
  Helping hand,
   A fam',
     Someone who can comprehend,
      My mind state and where it is,
       My life's plate is too much to digest,
        Hard to progress,
          Yet déjà vu, recycling life's unlearned messages,
           Led me right back again where I stand,
             But better,

This time I'm clever,
No, this time I rather than never say never again,
Why when these sad moments in life are inevitable,
So I might as well stick to it like Elmer's,
Glued my plans together,
Choosing to control what I can and remember,
That it's okay to hurt just don't reside there,
It's okay to be mad but don't hide there,
It's okay to be scared but don't become fear,
I've decided back then that I'm done being stuck there,
It sucks to upper cut the future conclusion of happiness finally being yours
    but... you're too scared to go there,
Scared like you feel you'll get it but worried about how long happiness will
be there,
  More prepared for the worst,
    Aren't we all but what if it DOES WORK OUT?
Why should I be built brick by brick by brick by doubt
    When God's already got my blueprint and it's all planned out,
He's always on time,

The One that's gotten me from good to great to better,
Allowing nothing but my best because my spiritual strength and family blood
    line are adapters and survivors on life's daring climb to the Most High,
I've seen me at my lowest but won't cry,
The come up was coming sooner,
It was destined.

Just blessings set in stone,
Same ones I've gracefully stepped on,
Stepping stones to greatness,
Gratitude is all I've known and I'm humble enough to say this,
Pain comes yet less than before,
It's okay I've accepted the challenge,
Once I'm back on track in life,
Feeling better will also feel awesome as ever.

Cold Conscience

If these pages could stand over you,
Shadowing your guilt,
Shake your thoughts and leave you brainless.

My Opinionated Fact

There are those who treat money,
Like an organ,
It makes them function, survive,
But their contemplating is off.

Right Next to His Gun

You love me,
But a part of me is missing,
So why do want something that's incomplete,
And no rhythm or beat,
Can guide what I lost back to me,
Back to the wall, asking the floors for answers,
And people observe me through a glass-like ceiling,
They assume my love life seems so appealing,
But once they know the real story and all of the feelings,
All of the assumptions consuming this room before me,
You'd suffocate like I do, resurrect in the morning,
And that's exactly what love is,
Feel live then die,
Ups and downs,
Friends to lovers,
Then back again,
Kissing and all that other shit,
One day I love you,
Then the next, "you on some other shit"
Wanna buy you the world,
But its hard cuz of the way its spins…
And we stay still,
Judging our relationship based on what others feel,
Wanting you, wanting you,
But making moves could really kill,
My friends say keep your heart,
Or else he'll make it his meal,
But on some real,
They only know my situation based on what they hear,
Losing you is most definitely one of my fears,
Wanna crown you, you're my king,
Calling you Man of the Year,
Get it crackin, Get it crackin,
And when I do, I have you here,
Protect ya gurl, you stay packing
When you need to vent, you got my ear,

When it comes to love making, you're never lacking,
The moment never disappears,

I made it complicated,
He kills it and confiscates it,
Love me, no, simply lust,
Left my heart here to rust,

Love, Lust, same difference,
Until you approach the shit,
And it reveals its appearance,
Clears the mist,
You finally see who's behind the lips,
Behind the sweetest kiss,
You love with your heart,
And he loves with his ___ ,
You too into you two,
Don't see it exists,
Then months later,
You see the his slick skin that held you tight,
With all his might,
Until he popped your spine before one last hiss,
Girls running around screaming love songs to the top of the lungs,
While the guys bragging about who they fucked,
Messed up but that's what it is,
Maybe not all men,
But a big percentage,
Concerned for my little brother,
But since I'm his big sis,
It makes sense,
That he'll be better than that,
Especially with momma snatchin nots in his ass,
Give a kid a message or the t.v. will,
Kick'em outta the hood or he'll stay put,
Until he's old as hell,
Watching his life laugh at him,
Thinking he was hood,
Tombstone left blank,

Few at the funeral,
Asking, "He was who???"
Snatch the coc', the remote, and name brand coat,
And give this boy a book before he turns into another hip hop joke,
Come back to the hood broke,
Thought the hood had your back,
But they spotted your shine, stole it, and left your ass in the dark,
Naw that won't be my brother,
Most definitely not goin,
Imma spit him some knowledge,
Tell him everything,
Bout the hood,
The adult world,
What he should,
These wild ass girls,
So he won't end up like his big sis,
Love, Lust, similar appearance,
Don't take notes from those in the street,
Be different.

I made it complicated,
He kills it and confiscates it,
Love me, no, simply lust,
Left my heart here to rust,

Got bored!?
I'd expect that,
You're not use to hearing truth,
And that's sad,
No, worse, PATHETIC,
You're spoon fed "reality" but you wanna gobble garbage,
Think that makes you a Goon, no you's a toon, who you been listening to?
Lame ass rappers calling themselves Goblins,
Your as brain dead as them, pick up your jaw, your steady slobbin,
Robbing people who are poor as your knowledge,
Yeah, I get deep like that,
Maybe I should come up with a tired ass rap,
With no concept,

Just a raw ass beat,
So my fans don't hear what I really said,
After every single word I spit I could end it with a "Ay" or a "Burr"
Then talk bout what I got and have a dude on there "sanging",
While the ecomony's failing,
How much "gwuap" I'm spending,
Gangsta as hell came from Youtube,
Screaming YOOOOOOOOOOUUULLL,
While in reality, this shit aint mine, I rented this jewelry,
Turn off your MTVs before you find out this crib don't belong to me,
Teacher ask Deshawn, "What you wanna be when you grow up?"
He says, "An Imitation G",
We allow the media make us believe,
   That I can't achieve unless I got bars or sell keys,
     That if I don't make this shot from the free throw line,
       That I'll stay in the hood, end up shot in the spine,
Momma screaming, "That's my baby, Lord don't take mine,"
You're gone cuz you was feeling that last rap line,
Now you're on your last life line,
  Because you had love for the streets,
   Love for the heat,
    Love for the "whateva" that wasn't guaranteed,
But that's love, right???
PLEASE!
Feel live then die,
But wait, you can't come back!
Ups and downs,
Won't happen to your life line,
Friends to lovers,
Well at least your mother loved you

I made it complicated,
He kills it and confiscates it,
Love me, no, simply lust,
Left my heart here to rust,
…..right next to his gun.

Distant from Hope

I wanna write…..
I wanna love,
And do it with honesty,
Bugging over the smallest thing,
Crying over nothing,
And it's my fault for not taking stands,
Anger and sadness stays within,
And I'm kin to Depression
Sister to Pain,
Mother of Sorrows,
Father of Nothings,
Carrier of dark glows,
Distant from hope,
And hard to swallow, yet, I gulp it down,
Like the shit in my past I never let out,
Trapped, Trapped,
No one hears my shackles,
Back broke from carrying my worries along with yours,
Sores from taking Life's tackles,
And now….I'm broken.
Shattered and splattered throughout the world from the darkest clouds
And just like God's storms
I feel like crying,
I feel like exploding,
I feel like throwing things to rid this ME that I am,
This ME has no happy aftermaths,
The smiles I have are false,
The laughter is a cover up
For when times are times so hear me laugh for eternity,
Solutions are as poor as the trickster who begs for change,
And change….oh, how I would love to change for the better but listen to me,
Listen to my redundant words and how they repeat and repeat and repeat and
How can I anyone love a soul that mistreats her own,
Denies her depression and puts a mask on,
Negativity feeds on my dome and when I want to run home….

It doesn't exist.
To you, it makes no sense, but picture this, a girl who lies about her true
feelings
Then when they began to burst, she asks for help and still gets hurt.
It's what I'm use to.
So, I'm gray, drained and have no hope to capture,
I want to write
I want to love
But I don't matter.

Just A Piece

So when you're sharing poetry,
These,
Are called,
Pieces.
So do I spit puzzle pieces that may possibly complete you,
Maybe even add my two cents to what you kind of knew,
Since pieces are little bits of change that's been overdue,
So here you are to splurge with an ear or two,
And all I gotta do is deposit knowledge past your mental bank limit,
Did he catch my drift,
  Or was the wave so swift,
   He became another victim and drowned up in it,
I don't know how when all this is...... is a piece,
So you took me as little.

Or am I spitting bars,
Fly like a Dove with words that Caress cuz I'm Sauve,
O'lay your mind with ease,
Or spike your insight with Old spice,

Cleansing old wounds, new scars,
Splitting the skin of your skull back to back wash your brain wash with a
brain storm Leaving you reprogrammed and all,
Whether this is spitting, drooling, or slob,
I've out-oceaned them all,
Doing damage to cleanse the way,
Katrina flood, not at all,
Just me, Audacious Don, spitting a piece.

Stealing Hope

Naw I'm good,
Looking at bad moments, they're trying to cuff my energy,
Take my days and turning them bad,
From a negative thing said, or not liking the way things went,
Driven mad from parallel parking into life's expectations, but I'm my own person,
I won't let a terrible moment rock the ground I stand on,
   And this is more than responding emotionally strong,
      But allowing things get to me, you know misery admires company,
So the weaker I allow myself to be the more misery crawls to me,
There's a power in thought and words can curse yourself,
So I'm not gonna count the multiple worries on the ground, instead I'm
    gonna praise the positives on the shelf,
Choosing to look up no matter the weight of my crown,
And yeah it's heavy and too big to fit but I believe I can grow into it,
Constantly curving my issues, finding new routes around the clownish down
   side,
Sticking it out through the storm, no matter the lightning, trembles or quakes,
Once I'm motivated to overcome issues, my mind won't shake,
No matter the stakes, I'll stay cleared minded, shine through dark clouds and
loud like a lion, roaring and rumble, even if I stumble, choke up and mumble
because my spirit is
   hungry, hear that grumble,
     if you blocking my blessing you asking for trouble,
Choosing to take control of my life,
Crawling out of the hole I'm in,
Staying unhappy never goes well for anyone and I know this,
So why not chase for better like from you it's been stolen.

That We Happened

These are my little moments,
These are my secrets to keep, and I hold them dearly, only setting them free
to paper for my eyes only,
Because as good as it could feel to show it on social media......I rather not
because it's makes our moments more meaningful.

It's the times when you're prepping your words before emotion sets in,
When your eyes are tear-filled explaining that you still love me regardless
  and how, the look you carried when you said I'm not ready for these vows,
And how your roar can be ferocious and scary but I admire it when you're
  protecting me,
Or how delicate you treat me sometimes even when you could come off
  angry,
And I'm learning you mean best.
You're still the best I've ever seen,
You're my light of happiness even when depression is after me,
You chase away my fears and lower my second guessing,
You make the strongest impressions on my heart, each day with you is a
  blessing,
Even moments when you're falling asleep.... and are still....I see the softness
that makes little me want to protect you,
Wanting to give you the joy you were never given over and over again,
To love someone this strongly and still have them as a friend,
With a love like yours so far I can't wait to see our future begin.

You are too wonderful to let go because you've left too much hope in my heart,
My second chance at many things at life,
A fiancee, a mother, and that's just the start,
But to finally, officially, be your wife,.... Lord knows I can't even imagine,
You gave me a more meaningful life, don't ever doubt it,
I'm so happy that we happened.

Dry Thought

She tries spitting sick lyrics but lives with dry thought,
Like she ought to plant seeds of motivation but she was never taught,
Taught how to brush through stuck moments that engulf her and like
hypothetical murder she usually kills it when it comes to creativity but now
ideas are dying.

Left high and dry without water and sunshine so there's no growth,
Only time she's planted is in her room alone,
Closed off and heart shutters at the sight of someone seeing through her fake
smiles and weak attempts to play happy,
More like Cry Now and Laugh Never,
What's funny about this hurt?
How can I joke about an invisible illness?
Who can I run to if I need love but my mind says retreat and
    don't burden others?
How am I suppose to keep going to work?
How do I keep trying to be their mother?
I feel like the weight I carry to open up to others would just be a bother,
To know I need medication is a hard pill to swallow,
Especially if that and therapy will eventually stop me from feeling so hallow.

Fame's Fangs

Scared of Fame showing its fangs,
Like if I decided to join it's game,
I'd risk being sedated, seduced, used up until I'm drained,
Knowing Hollywood isn't holy,
It'll eat you whole,
City full of plastics with no souls,
Scared to take off because I don't know where the world will take me,
Fear of the unknown,
Is a feeling I already know,
And I heard at the top you'll be alone,
A celebrity celebrating the creation of isolation,
From a plain lifestyle to a upscale location,
Vacate to places with smiling faces contrast to their trash spirits,
Psych you up to sign contracts of sinning,
You can be rich like Titanic but still sink in,
And media's the glacier,
Dissolve your innocence, promise cash but pay you cents.

Another Cornered Mouse

You have a "funny" definition of love.
Appearing admirable just to hold it over someone's head later,
You burn bridges like I wasn't your handrail,
Claim I'm your strength when you're down, putting pressure on me to be
    silent when you're emotionally abusive.

Your demolishing ways are stronger than what your love delivers,
Break me down more than you build me,
If your intentions are stitches then I'm bleeding over and over, re-opened
    because you always convince me to forgive you.
Play victim because self awareness is invisible to you,
Blame is the easy route,
I have to stay away to avoid your flames, hot headed dame, damsel putting
    herself in distress, cause yourself stress and say it's others fault,
I'm tired of getting head starts to reach others before you drag my name
    through the dirt,
You fool them everytime but not me.
They don't see the mother I have, the pressure, the void, the tension, the
    narcissistic sarcasm, the irrational reactions, the overreacting and non
      reacting, just the whole damn act!
The "never being good enough", "you missed a spot", "you
    could've/should've done it this way" like my way is always wrong,
The moments a child needs her mother the most but she taught you not to
    need her then wonder why you don't need her,
      The confusion in both,
The bothersome feeling of you waiting for the perfect moment to ruin our
    moment by "doing the most",
That's why I insist on distance because it's a better approach than
    approaching.

New Strength

Don't push me.
Don't encourage a raging poem,
You won't want it.
Don't stomp through big, bad, and bold,
Because I too could be cold,
Like the most harsh winters and you treading on thin ice,
I walk around with a injured wrist from damn near fallen, burned finger tips
from holding onto what use to be bridge until you burned it,
Leaving me no choice but to catch resentment-relentless-stitches,
Left twitching like a wounded bird trying to fly yet again you poke me with a
    stick,
First poke of "It's all your fault"
Second says "You ain't..." Shift from blaming yourself to blaming others
because you're gassed up and out irrationally quicker,
So I speak for all the wounded birds, him and her, who are tired of taking
narcissistic sissy's SHIT.
Tired of being the bigger "anything" while others sit emotionless,
Don't push me because I don't know how to quit.

Last One Maybe

Looking forward.
People usually look forward for things to come,
Yet the fragile strand of hope has been left..... in my past.

Somewhere along the line of my life, I've lost it, hope that is, and oh yes, the
    control of my mind like the devil holds the remote,
        in control of my soul, rewinding to my worst times,
            playing my defeat on repeat,
Pushing me to eject my last breathe,
Wishing God could mute my mind more often.

Begging God that I learn what moving forward feels like.
Feet barely hits the floor because I'm consumed by my bed,
    Tucked in tight by anxiety,
        Wet pillow from crying under my head,
            Dried grey trails from each eye,
                Watching my life pass me by.

It's not knowing what to do,
It's the "What's the points?" that barge in daily,
    Stomach growling for days,
        Haven't ate lately,
            Bathed lately,
                Hair dried and unkept,
No one sees my marathon of pain like You do.

I wish this could be my last depressed poem....
What would life even be afterwards?
Would I finally get to look forward, instead of going backwards?

To Be Seen, Not Heard

Like a difficult game of wheel of Fortune,
   I can barely get a word in,
You always interrupting, interjecting,
   Obliviously disrespectful,
Always giving a earful, then end it with "Respect your elders",
Leaving no room for someone to respond because it's more like your lecture,
Like you love the sound of your voice,
   And everyone else's is irrelevant,
Are you cocky or confident in your wisdom?
Wise or dumb or one sided,
But you decided before the conversation started that you're always right, and
   that's wrong,
If you think talking's your strength,
   You have a funny definition of "strong",
I hear "You questioning everyone" in your tone,
I mean what would happen if you actually listen to people more often?
Would your head explode?
You're set in your ways and I know,
Wish you could just leave some things alone,
Everything isn't personally wrapped around your world with a bow,
And no I'm sorry I don't have a fixation on dedicating my mindset to be
   concern about any and everything that could make you upset,
Chances are my priorities are alined with reality and no nonsense and no
   change to spare,
No changing my mind,
Or yours either for that matter.

Acquainted With a Ghost

How can you miss someone you've barely met?
To cure that, I imagine a ghost...
One who fills in spots where my family weren't present,
Like an imaginary friend or holiday reoccuring character,
Someone who's there to teach you through needed milestones,
  Like my art,
   I imagine them guiding my every brush stroke,
    I see past moments when I kept failing classes in school and them saying
     "me too",

I fathom a ghost that's relatable,
A reflection of me but without transparency,
A spirit gifted with magic to past down to me so I wouldn't have to learn the
hard way....
    ...the only way,

I forsee a future with them saying "You've come a long way",
I pretend,
I fake,
I LIE to myself that that ghost could've been there more often,
I cry out to the living, confessing that this ghost hurt more than it healed,
  but ironically I wish it was here,
I wish this ghost could answer my "Why's" instead of forcing my mother to
  answer,
I wish this ghost showed me more love I needed before he was taken by
  cancer,
I wish and I weep to the man who made up half of my character,
So when I don't act like my mom, I can say "Daddy, is this me being you?"
It's no wonder I was numb at the funeral,

In all I see that I carried on the Olympic flame you passed to me,
As you became ashes, I collect memories from your debris,
I am your daughter,
Your little creative artist,
Your twin,
I assumed with you in my life,
Things would've been easy,
Where's the fun in that?
My father wasn't a weak man,
And I came from him.

Talk Is Cheap

I know talk is cheap,
But my words are priceless,
So let me tell you where I'm coming from,

Let me give you something soft and sweet,
   After a hard day,
After you clock out, come home to me and see my valley's never had a
drought,
Take you in, slow and steady,
   Hot and Heavy,
     Making musical humming,
       Baby, keep it coming,
No tapping out unless my tongue say so,
Ménage à trois, me, you and my alter ego,
   And she knows,
       Your safe word won't save you from what's next,
         So let me show you where I'm coming from,
           Between my legs

Shock and surprise you with something different,
Release a little tension,
   Not to mention,
     Inch by inch,
       I may leave these sheets drenched,
         Never before have I felt like this,
           You giving me that Uber dick,
             Lyft me up, to saddle it,
               I'm no one trick pony,
                 My horsepower don't quit,
                   Those succulent lips are the next place I'm gonna sit,

And soon enough....you'll taste where I'm coming from,

Sweety I'll always aim to please,
Next time work has you beat,
Take it allll out on me,
   but not with words.....with action.....because talk is cheap.

Think Pink

She was drafted.
She was drafted into a battle,
And I walked for her,
  I cried for her,
    I lost her.

For numerous years, on and off,
She'd get that phone call she wish she didn't answer,
Face as if she's seen a ghost that overstays its welcome,
Eventually taking away the woman I loved giving her more pain than she could handle,
She soldiered on until she was no more, letting her spirit transfer,

I've ruminated on what's lead to this déjà vu disease,
It clinged to the strongest lady I've known,
4K walks and donations to cure a produced entity that serves another need,

Illnesses like common colds don't surface out of thin air,
There's a greed fixated on humanity and challenging its quantity,
Divide and conquer ain't enough nor incarceration,
Put the test in food, drinks, and cigarettes, once you're sick they act like they care,

Created foundations to cash in, water down the medicine,
Play God, rip families apart, claim its an unknown epidemic,
This pink ribbon is the pink slip the reaper delivers,
Hospitals making millions keeping the ill ignorant,

Everytime this lady went through remission, cancer ended,
Uncle Sam called again drafting her to a new mission,
1,2,3,4, What the hell are we dying for?
Henrietta Lacks to the max, we are their cure,
The world won't wish farewell to guerilla warfare,
    it's ambush galore,
My grandmother was caught in the crossfire,
    so hear my Pheonix roar,
I'll shapeshift these ashes into missels words form,
Leave a ringing in your ear after my sandstorm,
No foxhole can hide those who turned the diagnosed into deceased,
The ribbon in the sky disguised as a loose noose,
I don't want to think Pink,
You'll see,
    Karma's the greatest atomic bomb,

I enjoyed my last moments with you,
Every last bit even up until your soul lifted,
Days of bonding before you finally closed your eyelids,
I salute you.....
Despite how you passed on but honor how you lived,
Your smile, the fight in you,
    To me, in this world and the next, you'll always win,

She was drafted.
She was drafted into a battle,
And I walked for her,
    I cried for her,
        I lost her.

Acknowledgement

This book wouldn't exist without the motivation from my family, both immediate an distant. They have supported me through and through despite me being a difficult person I'm a strong enough to admit that. This book with its constant variety of ups and downs is literally a reflection of the interesting character I am and I can only thank God for blessing me with a understanding family with patience and wisdom. For all of my closest friends I've had in my lifetime, thank you for showing me who am I, and my current best friend for showing me there's still time to create a better me. To my future husband.....yes, I was something else and love you for accepting me flaws and all lol. (Ya'll know I had to be off topic and random).To my mentors for putting time and hope into me, you are practically family. I love you all and appreciate everyone's support for purchasing this book and seeing my in-person performances.